THE NAMES OF GOD

HIS CHARACTER REVEALED

A BIBLE STUDY BY

MELISSA SPOELSTRA

LEADER GUIDE

Abingdon Women

Nashville

The Names of God
His Character Revealed
Leader Guide

ISBN 978-1-5018-7810-7

20 21 22 23 24 25 26 27 28 29—10 9 8 7 6 5 4 3 2 1
MANUFACTURED IN THE UNITED STATES OF AMERICA

CONTENTS

ABOUT THE AUTHOR

Melissa Spoelstra is a popular women's conference speaker (including the Aspire Women's Events), Bible teacher, and author who is madly in love with Jesus and passionate about studying God's Word and helping women of all ages to seek Christ and know Him more intimately through serious Bible study. Having a degree in Bible theology, she enjoys teaching God's Word to the body of Christ, and traveling to diverse groups and churches across the nation and also to Nairobi, Kenya, for a women's prayer conference. Melissa is the author of the Bible studies *Romans: Good News That Changes Everything*, *Elijah: Spiritual Stamina in Every Season*, *Numbers: Learning Contentment in a Culture of More*, *First Corinthians: Living Love When We Disagree*, *Joseph: The Journey to Forgiveness*, and *Jeremiah: Daring to Hope in an Unstable World*, and the books *Dare to Hope*, *Total Family Makeover: 8 Practical Steps to Making Disciples at Home*, and *Total Christmas Makeover: 31 Devotions to Celebrate with Purpose*. She is a regular contributor to the Proverbs 31 First Five App and the Girlfriends in God online daily devotional. She has published articles in *ParentLife*, *Women's Spectrum*, and *Just Between Us* and writes her own regular blog in which she shares her musings about what God is teaching her on any given day. Melissa lives in Pickerington, Ohio, with her pastor husband, Sean, and their four kids: Zach, Abby, Sara, and Rachel.

Follow Melissa:

      @MelSpoelstra

      @Daring2Hope

      @Author MelissaSpoelstra

Her blog MelissaSpoelstra.com
        (check here also for event dates and booking information)

INTRODUCTION

It amazes me that we serve a God who has revealed Himself to us. He isn't hiding in the shadows or maintaining His distance from us. In fact, He desires to be known. One of the amazing ways He shows us His character is through His names!

God cannot be contained in just one identifier, so Scripture reveals His many names to help us draw nearer to Him. From the first words in the Bible to the final pages, we find God revealing His nature so we might know and trust Him more.

As you lead your group, I pray that women will learn names they may have never heard before. Perhaps this will be a first introduction to El Olam, the Everlasting God, or Yahweh Nissi, the Lord Our Banner. Others might be reminded of the power of more familiar names such as El Shaddai, Holy Spirit, and Jesus. My prayer for the women in your study is that learning about God's names will not be mere information, but will result in transformation as each one draws near to God with greater understanding. As we come to the last pages in the workbook, I hope that more than liking or not liking this particular study, we will be able to proclaim together, "Wow, what an incredible God we serve!"

About the Participant Workbook

Before the first session, you will want to distribute copies of the participant workbook to the members of your group. Be sure to communicate that they are to complete the first week of readings before your Week 1 session. (If you plan to have an Introductory Session, they will begin the homework after that.) Each week, five readings or lessons will combine study of Scripture with personal reflection and application (boldface type indicates write-in-the-book questions and activities). Each lesson ends with a "Talk with God" prayer suggestion.

On average, you will need about twenty to thirty minutes for each lesson. Completing these readings each week will prepare the women for the discussion and activities of the group session.

About This Leader Guide

As you gather each week with the members of your group, you will have the opportunity to watch a video, discuss and respond to what you're learning, and pray together. You will need access to a television and a DVD player with working remotes. (If you prefer, you may purchase streaming video files at www.Cokesbury. com, or you may access the videos for this study and other Abingdon Women Bible studies on AmplifyMedia.com through an individual or church membership.)

Creating a warm and inviting atmosphere will help to make the women feel welcome. Although optional, you might consider providing snacks for your first meeting and inviting group members to rotate in bringing refreshments each week.

This leader guide and the video will be your primary tools for leading your group on this journey through God's names. Whether you choose to follow this guide step by step, modify its contents to meet your group's needs and preferences, or simply peruse it to find a few helpful tips, questions, and ideas, you will find in these pages some valuable tools for creating a successful group experience.

> **Getting Started**: This is a list of strategies, options, and introductory information that will help you ensure good organization and communication. You will want to review this material and share relevant information with group members prior to your group session for Week 1, either via email or in an introductory session (see the Getting Started section). Or you might consider adding fifteen to thirty minutes to your first session for reviewing some of these important housekeeping details. Whichever option you choose, be sure that group members have the opportunity to purchase books and complete Week 1 before your session for Week 1.

> **Tips for Tackling Five Common Challenges**: This section includes ideas for addressing recurring issues that come up when leading a group. Every leader knows that some group dynamics can be difficult to tackle. What will you do when one person dominates the discussion or cuts off another person

who is speaking? All eyes will be on you to see how you will intervene or ignore these situations. Be sure to check out these five common challenges and ideas to help when you encounter them.

Basic Leader Helps: This list of basic leader tips will help you to prepare for and lead each group session.

Session Outlines: This guide contains six adaptable outlines to help guide your group time each week. Each begins with a "Leader Prep" section to assist with preparation.

This study is designed for six weeks, with an optional introductory session. Or, if desired, you may choose to extend the study to eight or twelve weeks (see the options included in Getting Started). Again, whichever option you choose, be sure that group members have the opportunity to purchase participant workbooks and complete Week 1 before your session for Week 1.

Each of the session outlines in this book may be used for a 60-minute, 90-minute, or 120-minute session. The following formats are offered as templates that you may modify for your group:

60-Minute Format
Welcome/Fellowship (2 minutes)
All Play (3–5 minutes)
Prayer/Video (25–30 minutes)
Group Discussion (20 minutes)
Prayer Requests (3 minutes)

90-Minute Format
Welcome/Fellowship (5–10 minutes)
All Play (3–5 minutes)
Prayer/Video (25–30 minutes)
Group Discussion (30 minutes)
Optional Group Activity (5–10 minutes)
Prayer Requests (5 minutes)

120-Minute Format
Welcome/Fellowship (10–15 minutes)
All Play (5–10 minutes)
Prayer/Video (25–30 minutes)

Group Discussion (30–35 minutes)
Optional Group Activity (10 minutes)
Prayer Requests (15–20 minutes)

As you can see, the basic elements remain the same in each format: a welcome/fellowship time, an "All Play" icebreaker question that everyone can answer, a video segment, group discussion, and prayer time. The 90-minute and 120-minute options offer longer times for fellowship, discussion, and prayer plus an optional group activity. If you choose not to do the group activity, you may add that time to another element of the session, such as group discussion or prayer. (See Getting Started for notes about including food, planning for childcare, and other important organizational details.)

If you are either new to leading Bible studies, or would like to have a framework to follow, or both, the session outlines will guide you. I have provided more discussion questions than you may have time to include. Before the session, choose the questions you want to cover and put a check mark beside them. Page references are provided for those questions that relate to questions or activities in the participant workbook. For these questions, invite group members to turn in their participant workbooks to the pages indicated.

If you are a seasoned group leader looking only for a few good questions or ideas, I encourage you to take what you want and leave the rest. After all, you know your group better than I do! Ask God to show you what areas to focus on from each week's homework and use my discussion outline as a template you can revise.

Of course, the Holy Spirit knows the content of this study (His Word) and the women in your group better than anyone else, so above all, I encourage you to lead this study under the Holy Spirit's direction, allowing yourself the freedom to make any changes or adaptations that are helpful or desirable.

I'm so excited that God has called you to lead a group of ladies through a study of the names of God. Know that I am praying for you and believing God for the work He will do through your leadership. Now, let's get started!

Melissa

GETTING STARTED

Before your study begins, be sure to review the following introductory information that will help you ensure good organization and communication. I encourage you to share relevant information such as the dates, times, and location for group meetings; when/where/how to purchase books; details regarding childcare and food; expectations and ground rules; and an overview of the study to group members. This can be covered during an introductory session or via e-mail before your session for Week 1.

1. Determine the length of your study. The basic study is designed for six weeks (plus an optional introductory session), but you also can plan for an eight- or twelve-week study.
   - For a six-week study—plus an additional (optional) introductory session if desired—use the session guides in this book and the video segments (DVD or streaming files). Be sure to distribute books during the introductory session (if you are having one) or prior to your group session for Week 1.
   - For an eight-week study, add both an introductory session and a closing celebration. In the introductory session, watch the introductory video message and spend time getting to know one another, presenting basic housekeeping information, and praying together (use the guide on pages 16–17). For a closing celebration, discuss what you have learned together in a special gathering that includes refreshments or perhaps a brunch, luncheon, or supper. A closing celebration provides an excellent opportunity for ongoing groups to invite friends and reach out to

others who might be interested in joining the group for a future study.

- To allow more time for completing homework, extend the study to twelve weeks. This is especially helpful for groups with mothers of young children or women carrying a heavy work or ministry schedule. With this option, women have two weeks in which to complete each week of homework in the participant workbook. In your group sessions, watch and discuss the video the first week; then review and discuss homework the next week. Some women find they are better able to complete assignments and digest what they are learning this way.

2. Determine the length of each group session (60, 90, or 120 minutes). See the format templates outlined on pages 7–8.

3. Decide ahead of time if you/your church will purchase participant workbooks that group members can buy in advance during an introductory session or in advance of your first session, or if group members will buy their own books individually. If you expect each member to buy her own book, e-mail group members purchasing information (be sure to note the cost, including tax and shipping if applicable). Consider including online links as well. Be sure to allow enough time for participants to purchase books and complete the readings for Week 1 prior to your group session for Week 1.

4. Create a group roster that includes each group member's name, e-mail address, mailing address, and primary phone number. (Collect this information through registration, e-mail, or an introductory session.) Distribute copies of the roster to group members prior to or during your first session. A group roster enables group members to stay connected and contact one another freely as needed, such as when taking a meal or sending a card to someone who is sick, who has missed several group sessions, or who has had a baby or is experiencing another significant life event. Group members may want to meet for coffee or lunch to follow up on things shared in the study as well. As women cry and laugh and share life together in a Bible study, their lives will be intertwined, even if for a short time.

5. Make decisions about childcare and food and communicate this information to group members in advance. Will childcare be offered, and will there be a cost associated with it? Will refreshments be served at your gatherings? (Note: If your group is meeting for 60 minutes, you

will not have time for a formal fellowship time with refreshments. You might consider having refreshments set up early and inviting women to come a few minutes before the session officially begins.) If you choose to have food, the introductory meeting is a good time to pass around a sign-up sheet. In the Bible study group I lead, we like to eat, so we have three women sign up to bring food for each meeting. One brings fruit, another brings bread or muffins, and another brings an egg dish. Your group may want to keep it simple; just be mindful of food allergies and provide choices.

6. Let group members know what to expect. Those who have never participated in a women's Bible study group may be intimidated, scared, or unsure of what to expect. Friends have told me that when they first came to Bible study, they were concerned they would be called on to pray out loud or expected to know everything in the Bible. Ease group members' concerns up front. Reassure the women that they will not be put on the spot and that they may choose to share as they are comfortable. Encourage participation while fostering a safe environment. Laying a few basic ground rules such as these can help you to achieve this kind of setting:

   • *Confidentiality*. Communicate that anything shared in the group is not to be repeated outside of those present in the study. Women need to feel safe to be vulnerable and authentic.

   • *Sensitivity*. Talk about courtesy, which includes practices such as refraining from interrupting, monopolizing, or trying to "fix" shared problems. Women want to be heard, not told what to do, when they share an issue in their lives. If they have advice to share with an individual, ask them to speak with the person privately after the study. When studying God's Word, some differences of opinion are bound to arise as to interpretation or application, or both. This is a good place to sharpen one another and respectfully disagree so that you may grow and understand different viewpoints. Remind the women that it's OK to question and see things differently; however, they must be kind and sensitive to the feelings of others.

   • *Purpose*. The primary reason you are taking time out of your busy schedules to meet together is to study the Bible. Though your group will pray for, serve, and support one another, your primary focus is to study the Bible. You learn in community from one another as you draw near to God through His Word. Though you may want to plan a service or social activity during the course of your study, these times should be secondary to your study time together. If group members express a desire for the group to do more outreach, service, or socials, gently remind them of the primary reason you gather.

7. Before the study begins, provide a short preview of the study's content, summarizing highlights in an e-mail or introductory session. You might whet the appetite for what is to come by sharing (or reading) parts of the introduction from the participant workbook. Consider sharing a personal story that relates to the study's theme. How have God's names stood out to you as you've read the Bible over the years? Which names of God are you most excited to study? When has one of God's names brought you encouragement, comfort, or conviction in a real-life circumstance? As you are enthusiastic about getting into God's Word together, your members will catch your contagious desire to see how the good news about Jesus resonates in their lives.

8. If you are having an introductory session, show the introductory video and open the floor for women to share in response to the questions on page 24.

9. Be sure to communicate to participants that they are to complete Week 1 in the participant workbook prior to your group session for Week 1. Review the options for study found in the introduction to the participant workbook and encourage participants to choose the options they plan to complete and then share this information with someone in the group for accountability.

TIPS FOR TACKLING FIVE COMMON CHALLENGES

Challenge #1: Preparation

Do you know that feeling when Bible study is in two days and you haven't even finished the homework, much less prepared for the group session? We've all been there. When I'm unprepared, I can sense the difference in how I teach Sunday school, lead VBS, or facilitate discussion in my women's Bible study group. I'm hurried, scattered, and less confident when I haven't dedicated the proper time for preparation. It doesn't take hours, but it does take commitment.

I check myself with a little acronym when I prepare to lead: S-S-S. Many years ago, I was asked to lead a segment on teacher training for a group of VBS leaders. I remember asking the Lord, "What are the most important things to remember when we handle your Word to teach?" As I sat listening, He gave me this process of S-S-S that has stuck with me through the years. It looks like this:

S—**Savior**. Know your Savior. We must spend time talking, listening, and staying closely connected with Jesus in order to lead well. As we intentionally keep our walk with Him close and vibrant, we can then hear His voice about how to structure our lesson, what questions to ask, and which verses in His Word to focus on.

S—**Story**. Know your story. Though God has been gracious to me when I have winged it, I feel the most freedom with God's truth when I have prepared thoroughly. Try not to cram in multiple days of homework at one time. Let it sink into your soul by reading curiously and slowly. Go back to areas that especially strike you and allow God to use His Word in your heart and mind so that you can teach with authenticity. Women can tell when you are flying by the seat of your pants.

S—Students. Know your students. Who are these women God has given you to shepherd? Are they struggling with finances, relationships, or body image issues? Are they mature Christ-followers who need to be challenged to go deeper in their study of God's Word, or are they seekers who need extra explanation about where the books of the Bible are located? Most likely, you will be teaching to a wide range of backgrounds as well as emotional and spiritual maturity levels, and you will need God's wisdom and guidance to inspire them.

Challenge #2: Group Dynamics

Have you experienced that uncomfortable feeling when you ask a discussion question and a long silence settles over the group? With your eyes begging someone to break the ice, you wonder if you should let the question linger or jump in with your own answer. Other problems with group dynamics surface when Silent Suzy never contributes to the conversation because Talking Tammy answers every question. What does a good leader do in these situations? While every group has a unique vibe, I have found these general concepts very helpful in facilitating discussion:

First of all, a good leader asks questions. Jesus was our greatest example. He definitely taught spiritual truths, but one of His most effective methods was asking questions. Proverbs 20:5 says, "Though good advice lies deep within the heart, / a person with understanding will draw it out." As leaders, we must be intentional askers and listeners. I try to gauge myself throughout the discussion by reflecting often on this simple question: "Am I doing all the talking?" When I find I am hearing my own voice too much, I make a point to ask and listen more. Even if waiting means a little silence hangs in the air, eventually someone will pipe up and share. Women learn from one another's insights and experiences; we rob them of others' wisdom when we monopolize as leaders.

Now what about Talking Tammy? She not only answers every question but also makes a comment after each woman shares something (often relating to one of her own experiences). Try one of these transitional statements:

- "Thanks Tammy, let's see if someone else has some insight as well."
- Let's hear from someone who hasn't shared yet today."
- "Is there anyone who hasn't talked much today who would be willing to answer this question?"

The hope is Talking Tammy will realize that she has had a lot of floor time.

Sometimes Talking Tammy also struggles to "land the plane." She can't find a stopping place in her story. Help her out by jumping in when she takes a breath and make a summary statement for her. For example, "I hear you saying that you could relate to God's name Yahweh Sabaoth because you've faced many challenges in life. Does anyone else find this name of God resonating in a similar way?" Occasionally, I have had to take someone aside in a loving way and address her amount of talking. Pray hard and be gentle, but address the issue. As a leader, you must keep in mind the good of the group as a whole.

I once had several ladies leave the group because they were so frustrated by the continual barrage of talking by one woman in particular. Some of her many comments were insensitive and offensive to others in the room. I don't like confrontation, so I didn't want to address it. However, God grew me as a leader to speak loving truth, even when it hurts, for the benefit of those we are called to shepherd.

Sometimes even more challenging than Talking Tammy is Silent Suzy. We must walk a fine line as leaders, not putting on the spot those women who are uncomfortable talking in front of others. I have scared women away by being too direct. So how do we get Silent Suzy to talk without singling her out? Here are some ideas:

- If she is new to the study, don't push her at all during the first few sessions. Let her feel safe and get comfortable. Never call on her to pray out loud or single her out with a pointed question. I once said, "I want to know what Suzy thinks about this." All eyes turned on her, and I'll never forget the tears welling in the corners of her eyes as she said she wasn't comfortable being called on. She didn't come back to the group after that incident. How I wish I could have taken those words back. I learned a valuable lesson from that Silent Suzy: don't push!
- Listen with recall as she answers the All Play question that everyone is asked to answer. Watch for an opportunity to talk about something she has shared by asking a follow-up question that doesn't pry.
- Take her out for coffee and get to know her. With time, she might warm up and begin to contribute to the discussion. Through a deepened

relationship, you'll get a better read on whether you should encourage her to talk.

Challenge #3: Prayer Requests

How often do we run out of time when sharing prayer requests, leaving us no time to actually pray? How do you handle those women who aren't comfortable praying out loud? What if your group has fifteen to thirty women, and just listening to everyone's prayer request takes half an hour?

It's so important to take the time to hear what is going on in one another's lives and to pray for one another. Here are some creative ideas I have learned from others to help keep prayer time fresh:

- As women enter the room, direct them to take an index card or sticky note and write their prayer request on it. Then during prayer time, each woman can read her request aloud, already having thought through it, and pass it to the woman on the right for her to keep in her Bible as a reminder to pray for the request until they meet again.
- Ask someone to record all the prayer requests and e-mail them to the group each week.
- If you have a small group, use a one- or two-minute hourglass when you are short on time. (Look in your game closet for one of these.) Lightheartedly tell each woman that she has one or two minutes to share her request so that each woman can have a turn. (You might want to flip it over again if tears accompany the request.)
- If you have more than ten women, divide into two or three groups for prayer time. Assign a leader who will facilitate, keep the group on track, and follow up. Sometimes our prayer group has gone out for breakfast together or gathered in someone's home to watch the teaching video again.
- Have women pick one or two partners and split into small groups of two or three to share prayer requests and pray for one another.
- Have an open time of "popcorn" prayer. This means letting women spontaneously pray one-sentence prayers as they feel led.
- After everyone shares requests, ask each woman to pray for the woman on her right. Clearly say that if anyone is uncomfortable praying out loud, she can pray silently and then squeeze the hand of the woman next to her to signal it is her turn to pray.

- Another option is to close the group in prayer yourself or ask a few women you know are comfortable praying in front of others to pray for the requests mentioned. Remember that many women feel awkward praying in front of others. Provide encouragement by reminding the group that prayer is talking to God and that there is no right or wrong way to have a conversation with our Creator. But, always be sensitive to others and affirm that they will not be judged if they don't like to pray out loud.
- Making an occasional change in your prayer time keeps it from becoming routine or boring. Talking with Jesus should be fresh and real. Taking an intentional, thoughtful approach to this important time of your study will add great value to your time together.

Challenge #4: Developing Leaders

Women's Bible study groups are a great avenue for fulfilling the 2-2-2 principle, which comes from 2 Timothy 2:2: "You have heard me teach things that have been confirmed by many reliable witnesses. Now teach these truths to other trustworthy people who will be able to pass them on to others." As a leader, God calls us to help raise up other leaders.

Is there a woman in your group who is capable of leading? How can you come alongside her and help equip her to be an even better leader? Wonderful women have invested in me through the 2-2-2 principle, even before I knew that term. As an apprentice, I watched them lead. They gave me opportunities to try leading without handing the full reins over to me. Then they coached and corrected me. I have since had the privilege of mentoring several apprentices in my Bible study group and watching them go on to lead their own groups. This is multiplying leaders and groups, and God loves it!

Here is the 2-2-2 principle as laid out by Dave and Jon Ferguson in their book *Exponential.*[1] (My notes are added within the brackets.)

- I DO. You WATCH. We TALK.
- I DO. You HELP. We TALK. [*Have your apprentice lead a prayer group or an activity or portion of the session.*]
- You DO. I HELP. We TALK. [*Ask your apprentice to lead one session with you assisting with facilitation alongside her.*]
- You DO. I WATCH. We TALK. [*Give your apprentice full ownership for leading a session and resist the urge to jump in and take over.*]

- You DO. Someone else WATCHES. [*As God leads over time, encourage your apprentice to start her own Bible study group.*]

My mentor and I led a Bible study group together for years. As the group grew larger, we both sensed God leading us to multiply the group, forming two groups. It was painful as we missed studying and working with each other. However, God blessed and used both groups to reach more women. Then a woman in my group felt called to lead her own study. She worried that no one would come to her group. She asked many questions as we worked through the 2-2-2 principle. Her first group meeting included eighteen women who now, five years later, still love meeting together. I've seen pictures of them on Facebook enjoying special times together, and I praise God for all that He is doing.

From our one study there are now over five groups of women that meet regularly to study God's Word. This kind of growth begins with commitment to share leadership, follow the 2-2-2 principle, and multiply so that more women can grow in their walk with Christ. Don't miss the opportunity to develop new leaders with intentionality as you model and encourage other women to use their gifts.

Challenge #5: Reaching Out

How do you welcome new women into the group? This is especially tough if yours is an ongoing group that has had the same women in it for years. Newcomers can feel like outsiders if it seems like everyone already knows the unspoken rules of the group. Also, what about those who are finding their way back to God? Are they welcome in the group? While the purpose of the group is primarily Bible study, I've seen the Great Commission of making disciples happen many times through women's groups that meet for Bible study. God's Word will do the transforming work in their lives through the Holy Spirit. We are called to reach out by investing and inviting. Here are some ways a leader can help create an open group:

- End each Bible study with a closing celebration brunch, encouraging the women to bring food and friends. Some ideas for this time together include:
  1. Have an open time when women can share how God worked in their lives through the Bible study.
  2. Have one woman in the group share her testimony of how she came to understand the gospel and how it has been transforming her life recently.
  3. Bring in a speaker from outside the group to share a testimony.

4. Make it fun! We play a fun group game (such as Fishbowl, Pictionary, or Loaded Questions) and have a white elephant jewelry exchange at Christmas. Women who might think Bible study is a foreign concept can see that you are just a bunch of regular women in pursuit of a supernatural God.

- Leave an empty chair in the group and pray for God to show you someone who needs a group of women she can study the Bible alongside.

- Though the main purpose of the group is Bible study, consider doing a service project together and invite other women to participate (schedules permitting). Our group has made personal care bags for the homeless and also adopted a family at Christmas, which included going shopping for the gifts and wrapping them together. Depending on where God is leading your group, serving together can help put hands and feet to the truths you are learning.

- Socials outside of Bible study also provide an opportunity to invite friends as a nonthreatening transition. While the focus of your group is much more than social, planning an occasional fun event can be a good way to forge deeper connections. Our Bible study group has gone bowling together, had a backyard barbecue, and planned a girls' night out at a local restaurant. These times together not only help women get to know one another better, but also give women a great chance to invite friends. These same friends who attend a social event might later try a Bible study session once they have made connections with some of the women in the group.

BASIC LEADER HELPS

Preparing for the Sessions

- Check out your meeting space before each group session. Make sure the room is ready. Do you have enough chairs? Do you have the equipment and supplies you need? (See the list of materials needed in each session outline.)
- Pray for your group and each group member by name. Ask God to work in the life of every woman in your group.
- Read and complete the week's readings in the participant workbook and review the session outline in the leader guide. Put a check mark beside the discussion questions you want to cover, and in the margins, make notes about information or insights you want to share in your discussion time.

Leading the Sessions

- Personally greet each woman as she arrives. If desired, take attendance using your group roster. (This will assist you in identifying members who have missed several sessions so that you may contact them and let them know they were missed.)
- At the start of each session, ask the women to turn off or silence their cell phones.
- Always start on time. Honor the efforts of those who are on time.

- Encourage everyone to participate fully, but don't put anyone on the spot. Invite the women to share as they are comfortable. Be prepared to offer a personal example or answer if no one else responds at first.
- Facilitate but don't dominate. If you talk most of the time, group members may tend to listen passively rather than engage personally.
- Try not to interrupt, judge, or minimize anyone's comments or input.
- Remember that you are not expected to be the expert or have all the answers. Acknowledge that all of you are on this journey together, with the Holy Spirit as your leader and guide. If issues or questions arise that you don't feel equipped to answer or handle, it's OK to say, "I don't know." Talk with the pastor or a staff member at your church and circle back with the women later to share what you discovered.
- Encourage good discussion, but don't be timid about calling time on a particular question and moving ahead. Part of your responsibility is to keep the group on track. If you decide to spend extra time on a given question or activity, consider skipping or spending less time on another question or activity in order to stay on schedule.
- Try to end on time. If you are running over, give members the opportunity to leave if they need to. Then wrap up as quickly as you can.
- Be prepared for some women to want to hang out and talk at the end. If you need everyone to leave by a certain time, communicate this at the beginning of the session. If you are meeting in a church during regularly scheduled activities or have arranged for childcare, be sensitive to the agreed-upon ending time.
- Thank the women for coming, and let them know you're looking forward to seeing them next time.

INTRODUCTORY SESSION

Note: The regular session outline has been modified for this optional introductory session, which is 60 minutes long.

Leader Prep

Materials Needed

- *The Names of God* DVD and DVD player or equipment to stream the video online
- Stick-on name tags and markers (optional)
- Index cards (optional—Prayer Requests)
- Participant workbooks to purchase or distribute

Session Outline

Note: Refer to the format templates on pages 7–8 for suggested time allotments.

Welcome

Offer a word of welcome to the group. If time allows and you choose to provide food, invite the women to enjoy refreshments and fellowship. (Groups meeting for 60 minutes may want to have a time for food and fellowship before the official start time.) Be sure to watch the clock and move to the All Play icebreaker at the appropriate time.

All Play

Ask group members to share their names. Then ask each person to tell what her name means (if she knows) and any special significance associated with her name. (For example, she may mention being named after a family member, famous person, biblical character, and so forth.)

Distribute the participant workbooks, and then have the group turn to the introduction. Point out the different options for study (pages 9–10) and encourage each woman to prayerfully decide which level of study she would like to complete.

Prayer/Video

Ask God to prepare the group to be receptive and hear His voice. Play the Introductory Video. Invite participants to complete the Video Viewer Guide for the Introductory Session in the participant workbook as they watch (page 11). (Answers are provided on page 205 of the participant workbook or page 61 of this leader guide.)

Group Discussion

Discuss:

- Which names of God did you recognize in the video?
- What insights or questions did this introductory video raise for you?
- How does the law of first mention apply to our study of the names of God? (You may need to explain the concept again.)
- Read Psalm 9:10 and Psalm 115:1 aloud in unison. How can knowing God's names help us trust Him more?
- What do you hope to learn or gain from this study?

Prayer Requests

End by inviting group members to share prayer requests and pray for one another. Use index cards, popcorn prayer, or another prayer technique included in Tips for Tackling Five Common Challenges (pages 13–19) to lead this time with intentionality and sensitivity.

Week 1
EL (PART I)

Hashem, Elohim, El Elyon, El Roi

Leader Prep

Memory Verse

> Honor the LORD for the glory of his name.
>   Worship the LORD in the splendor of his holiness.
>   (Psalm 29:2)

Materials Needed

- *The Names of God* DVD and DVD player or equipment to stream the video online
- Stick-on name tags and markers (optional)
- Index cards or sticky notes (optional—Scriptures and Prayer Requests)

Session Outline

Note: Refer to the format templates on pages 7–8 for suggested time allotments.

Welcome

Offer a word of welcome to the group. If time allows and you choose to provide food, invite the women to enjoy refreshments and fellowship. (Groups meeting for 60 minutes may want to have a time for food and fellowship before the official start time.) Be sure to watch the clock and move to the All Play icebreaker at the appropriate time.

All Play

Ask each group member to respond briefly to the following prompt:

- *What is a nickname you've been called in the past?*

After everyone has shared, say something like this:

> *Sometimes our family members, friends, or even coaches have referred to us using nicknames, but each of us has a given name on our birth certificate. God has no beginning or end, so there is no paper certifying the day of His origin. Yet, He has revealed His names to us so we can have a deeper relationship with Him. We found that His name is not to be misused. Instead, it is a source of power and a way to worship Him. Let's pray to the Lord as we get started today.*

Prayer/Video

Ask God to prepare the group to receive His Word and hear His voice. Play the video for Week 1. Invite participants to complete the Video Viewer Guide for Week 1 in the participant workbook as they watch (page 41). (Answers are provided on page 205 of the participant workbook or page 61 of this leader guide.)

Group Discussion

VIDEO DISCUSSION QUESTIONS

- Have you experienced a season when it seemed like God wasn't interested in your situation? How does the statement "God cares about what you care about because God cares about you" encourage you today?
- God is Elohim. How does knowing that you are made in His image change the way you think about yourself?

Where might God be asking you to zoom out to see the bigger picture of what He is doing in your life?

In what situation might the Lord want you to zoom in on the details and embrace the truth that He is El Roi, the God Who Sees?

PARTICIPANT WORKBOOK DISCUSSION QUESTIONS

Note: Page references are provided for those questions that relate to questions or activities in the participant workbook.

Before you begin, invite volunteers to look up the following Scriptures and be prepared to read them aloud when called upon. You might want to write each of the Scripture references on a separate index card or sticky note that you can hand out.

Scriptures: Genesis 1:26-27; 16:11-16; Exodus 20:7; Isaiah 52:6;
Colossians 1:15-16; Hebrews 7:15-17

Day 1: Hashem

- What is the meaning of your name? (page 14)
- Have someone read aloud Exodus 20:7. What are some practical ways we can honor God's name rather than misuse it?
- Of the encouraging verses on pages 16–17, which one most resonates with you? Why?
- Have someone read aloud Isaiah 52:6. In what ways do you believe God wants us to experience power through His name?
- Ask a few individuals to share how they filled in the statement of belief on page 17. You may want to share your statement to get the discussion going.

Day 2: Elohim—Creator

- Share about something you have created (a meal, a DIY project, or a design for work). (page 19)
- Have someone read aloud Genesis 1:26-27. If you really were to view yourself as made in the image of God, how would that affect your self-talk and confidence level? (page 20)
- Of the verses you looked up regarding how Elohim sees you, what encouraged you most? Why? (pages 20–21)

- Ask if a few individuals would be willing to share how they filled in the statement of belief on page 22.

Day 3: Elohim—The Strong One

  In your experience, what contributes most to relationships moving from shallow to deep?

- Have someone read aloud Colossians 1:15-16. Who was involved in Creation? (page 24)

 Review the words omniscient, omnipotent, and omnipresent. What have you learned about God's supernatural abilities from studying these terms? Which one is most significan to you, and why?

- How can seeing God's might and power in the name Elohim change your perspective toward your problems right now? (page 26)
- Ask if a few individuals would be willing to share how they filled in the statement of belief on page 27.

Day 4: El Elyon—God Most High

Can you think of a time when you were able to accomplish something when the odds were not in your favor? If so, describe it briefly. (page 28)

- What did you learn about Abram's character from your study of Genesis 14:1-16? (page 29)
- In light of El Elyon's ability to deliver Abram, what encouragement or new perspective did you gain in regard to your own present battles? (page 30)
- Have someone read aloud Hebrews 7:15-17. What connection is there between Christ and Melchizedek? (page 32) What questions do you have about this?
- Ask if a few individuals share how they filled in the statement of belief on page 32.

Day 5: El Roi—The God Who Sees Me

- Have someone read Genesis 16:11-16 aloud. How does knowing that God saw Hagar and established His name as El Roi, the God Who Sees Me, bring you hope today?
- How did you answer any of these questions in your study guide:
- In your circumstances: What is going on in your life right now?
- In your emotions: What word describes your feelings today?
- In this season: What is currently your most important task? (page 37)

If an angel appeared before you today and asked you where you are headed, what would your answer be? (page 37)

- Invite women to share how they filled in the statement of belief on page 38.

 Of all the names we covered this week, which one most resonated with you? Why?

- Ask if anyone would like to recite the memory verse or share how it impacted her personally.

Optional Group Activity (for a session longer than 60 minutes)

Divide into smaller groups or pairs to review the Weekly Wrap-up (pages 39–40). Ask small groups to share and discuss these statements. Also ask them to share one or two ways they will put into practice something they learned from their readings this week.

Prayer Requests

Invite the group members to share prayer requests and pray for one another. Use index cards or sticky notes, popcorn prayer, or another prayer technique included in Tips for Tackling Five Common Challenges (pages 13–19) to lead this time with intentionality and sensitivity.

Week 2

EL (PART 2)

El Shaddai, El Olam, El-Elohe-Israel, El Chay

Leader Prep

Memory Verse

> *Those who live in the shelter of the Most High [El Elyon]*
> *will find rest in the shadow of the Almighty [El Shaddai].*
> *This I declare about the LORD:*
> *He alone is my refuge, my place of safety;*
> *he is my God, and I trust him.*
>
> (Psalm 91:1-2)

Materials Needed

- The *Names of God* DVD and DVD player or equipment to stream the video online
- Stick-on name tags and markers (optional)
- Index cards or sticky notes (optional—Scriptures and Prayer Requests)

Session Outline

Note: Refer to the format templates on pages 7–8 for suggested time allotments.

Welcome

Offer a word of welcome to the group. If time allows and you choose to provide food, invite the women to enjoy refreshments and fellowship. (Groups meeting for 60 minutes may want to have a time for food and fellowship before the official start time.) Be sure to watch the clock and move to the All Play icebreaker at the appropriate time.

All Play

Ask each group member to respond briefly to the following prompt. Read aloud or paraphrase:

> *This week we saw that God is all-sufficient in our lives.*

> - *What is something you have stockpiled in your home for future use?*

After everyone has shared, say:

> *Whether you have a large supply of toilet paper or towels, we serve a God who is sufficient to meet our every need.*

Prayer/Video

Ask God to prepare the group to receive His Word and hear His voice. Play the video for Week 2. Invite participants to complete the Video Viewer Guide for Week 2 in the participant workbook as they watch (page 74). (Answers are provided on page 205 of the participant workbook or page 61 of this leader guide.)

Group Discussion

Video Discussion Questions

- How has El Shaddai provided relationships in your life? Share the name of one person you are grateful for right now as a gift from God.
- How have you seen God's provision in meeting physical needs?
- How is the Lord calling you to receive mercy today?
- What blessings can you recognize as coming from El Shaddai?
- In light of God's sufficiency, how can you pursue greater dependency?

Participant Workbook Discussion Questions

Note: Page references are provided for those questions that relate to questions or activities in the participant workbook.

Before you begin, invite volunteers to look up the following Scriptures and be prepared to read them aloud when called upon. You might want to write each of the Scripture references on a separate index card or sticky note that you can hand out.

Scriptures: Genesis 17:1-8; 21:22-34; 32:22-32; 33:18-20; Joshua 4 (broken up into six verses each); Job 40:1-5; Hebrews 11:8-16

Day 1: El Shaddai—All-Sufficient One

- Share what you recorded as your signature "thing" (recipe, style, ability, accomplishment) on page 43. Who or what deserves much of the credit for your signature thing?
- Take a moment to reflect on the truth that God is enough. In what ways do you have enough today because of the provision of El Shaddai? (page 44)
- Have someone read aloud Genesis 17:1-8. Share any past or current situations where you have tried to fix things your own way and then realized your need to stop working, cling to God, and wait for His timing. (pages 45–46)
- Ask if a few individuals would be willing to share which belief statement they starred or how they filled in their own statement of belief on page 47.

Day 2: El Shaddai—Promise Keeper

- What were some unfulfilled promises you recorded on page 48?
- What is an example of a macro and micro waiting experience in your life? (page 50)
- Have someone read Hebrews 11:8-16 out loud. What do you learn about God's promises?
- Have someone read Job 40:1-5 out loud. As you sit in awe of the Almighty, how does the response of Job resonate with you? (page 53)
- Ask if a few individuals would be willing to share their statement of belief on pages 53–54.

Day 3: El Olam—Everlasting God

- What are some of the things that have been getting your attention lately? (page 55)
- Have someone read aloud Genesis 21:22-34. What stood out most about God's name El Olam?
- As you reflect on your own personal spiritual history, how have you seen God reveal Himself over time?
- Ask if a few individuals would be willing to share their statement of belief on page 58.

Day 4: El-Elohe-Israel—The God of Me

- Have someone read aloud Genesis 32:22-32. You may not have been wrestling with God physically in the form of a person, but have you been wrestling through any aspects in your relationship with Him lately? If so, what are they? (page 62)
- Have someone read Genesis 33:18-20 out loud. What does this name reveal about Jacob's view of God?
- Which verse on page 64 did you put a star next to as the one that most resonates with you?
- Ask if a few individuals would be willing to share their statement of belief on page 65.

Day 5: El Chay—Living God

- What are some things that make you feel alive? (page 67)
- Have four women read six verses each from Joshua 4. What are some things that help you remember the Living God during "winter" seasons of faith? (page 69)
- Ask a few individuals if they would be willing to share their statement of belief on page 71.
- As you look back over the entire week, which names of God have resonated most with you, and why?
- Ask if anyone would like to recite the memory verse or share how it impacted her personally.

Optional Group Activity (for a session longer than 60 minutes)

Divide into smaller groups or pairs to review the Weekly Wrap-up (pages 72–73). Ask small groups to share and discuss their wrap-up statements and one or two ways they will put into practice something they learned from their readings this week.

Prayer Requests

Invite the group members to share prayer requests and pray for one another. Use index cards or sticky notes, popcorn prayer, or another prayer technique included in Tips for Tackling Five Common Challenges (pages 13–19) to lead this time with intentionality and sensitivity.

Week 3

YAHWEH (PART 1)

Yahweh Elohim, Yahweh Yireh, Yahweh Rapha, Yahweh Nissi

Leader Prep

Memory Verse

God also said to Moses, "Say this to the people of Israel: Yahweh, the God of your ancestors—the God of Abraham, the God of Isaac, and the God of Jacob—has sent me to you.

This is my eternal name,
my name to remember for all generations."

(*Exodus 3:15*)

Materials Needed

- The Names of God DVD and DVD player or equipment to stream the video online
- Stick-on name tags and markers (optional)
- Index cards or sticky notes (optional—Scriptures and Prayer Requests)

Session Outline

Note: Refer to the format templates on pages 7–8 for suggested time allotments.

Welcome

Offer a word of welcome to the group. If time allows and you choose to provide food, invite the women to enjoy refreshments and fellowship. (Groups meeting for 60 minutes may want to have a time for food and fellowship before the official start time.) Be sure to watch the clock and move to the All Play icebreaker at the appropriate time.

All Play

Ask each group member to respond briefly to the following prompt. Read aloud or paraphrase:

This week we learned about Yahweh, the self-existent One.

- *What is the oldest item you own?*

After everyone has shared, say:

Everything we have was created at some point, yet Yahweh has no beginning or end. He has always been and always will be!

Prayer/Video

Ask God to prepare the group to receive His Word and hear His voice. Play the video for Week 3. Invite participants to complete the Video Viewer Guide for Week 3 in the participant workbook as they watch (pages 107). (Answers are provided on page 205 of the participant workbook or page 61 of this leader guide.)

Group Discussion

VIDEO DISCUSSION QUESTIONS

- The Amalekites targeted the Israelites when they were weary. What challenges have presented themselves in your life during a weary season?
- What is a physical object that has represented spiritual truth to you?

- What are some tangible ways the Lord has helped you in the past? What are some creative ways you can remember it, dwell on it, and talk about it this week?
- Name one or two spiritual friends who have supported you in seeking the Lord.

PARTICIPANT WORKBOOK DISCUSSION QUESTIONS

Note: Page references are provided for those questions that relate to questions or activities in the participant workbook.

Before you begin, invite volunteers to look up the following Scriptures and be prepared to read them aloud when called upon. You might want to write each of the Scripture references on a separate index card or sticky note that you can hand out.

Scriptures: Genesis 22:1-19; Exodus 3:1-15; 15:22-27; 17:8-16; Psalm 19; Hebrews 13:8

Day 1: Yahweh Elohim—Unchanging God

- What dangers have you observed or personally encountered from overemphasizing one aspect of God's character without the balance of another aspect? (page 79)
- Have someone read aloud Psalm 19. What differences do you notice in the verses referring to Elohim and Yahweh? (page 81)
- Have someone read Hebrews 13:8 out loud. What does this verse tell us about God's character? How does that characteristic of God encourage you today?
- Ask if a few individuals would be willing to share their statement of belief on page 81.

Day 2: Yahweh—The Self-Existent One

- Where were you born? If you have been told any stories about that day, share one briefly with the group.
- Have someone read Exodus 3:1-15. In these verses, what stands out to you?
- What gifts or abilities are you currently using to serve God? (page 85)

- What does the expression "I AM" reveal about God's character? (page 86) How would you fill in this blank today: "I need to hear God saying I AM _____."
- Ask if a few individuals would be willing to share their statement of belief on pages 86–87.

Day 3: Yahweh Yireh—The Lord Will Provide

- As you reflect on your life, how have you seen Yahweh Yireh provide in your life? Share one or two examples that stand out. (page 88)
- Have someone read aloud Genesis 22:1-19. What thoughts or insights do you have regarding the first mention of Yahweh Yireh in the Bible?
- What are you asking God to provide in your life currently? (page 90)
- What are some things you wrote on your thankful rocks on page 91?
- Ask if a few individuals would be willing to share their statement of belief on page 92.

Day 4: Yahweh Rapha—The Lord Who Heals You

- What situations or questions come to mind when you think about healing? (page 93)
- Have someone read aloud Exodus 15:22-27. What stands out to you about this encounter? (page 95)
- How have times of testing in your life helped you to learn more about God, strengthen your faith, or develop your character? (page 97)
- Where do you need healing right now? How does knowing God's name Yahweh Rapha encourage you today?
- Ask if a few individuals would be willing to share their statement of belief on page 98.

Day 5: Yahweh Nissi—The Lord Our Banner

- Have you ever experienced a mental, spiritual, or emotional battle during a particularly weary season in life? Share anything you recorded on page 99.
- Have someone read aloud Exodus 17:8-16. The Israelites were attacked in weak moments. What are some temptations you face in your weak moments? (page 100)
- Who has directed you to Jesus and supported you in some of your challenges in life? (page 102)

- What notes did you make in response to the questions in the BLOOM section of today's lesson? (page 104)
- As you look back over the entire week, what names of God have resonated most with you, and why?
- Ask if anyone would like to recite the memory verse or share how it impacted her personally.

Optional Group Activity (for a session longer than 60 minutes)

Divide into smaller groups or pairs to review the Weekly Wrap-up (pages 105–106). Ask small groups to share and discuss their wrap-up statements and one or two ways they will put into practice something they learned from their readings this week.

Prayer Requests

Invite the group members to share prayer requests and pray for one another. Use index cards or sticky notes, popcorn prayer, or another prayer technique included in Tips for Tackling Five Common Challenges (pages 13–19) to lead this time with intentionality and sensitivity.

Week 4

YAHWEH (PART 2)

Yahweh Shalom, Yahweh Sabaoth,
Yahweh Raah, Yahweh Tsidkenu,
Yahweh Shammah

Leader Prep

Memory Verse

> Your name, O LORD, endures forever;
>   your fame, O LORD, is known to every generation.
>   (Psalm 135:13)

Materials Needed

- The Names of God DVD and DVD player or equipment to stream the video online
- Stick-on name tags and markers (optional)
- Index cards or sticky notes (optional—Scriptures and Prayer Requests)

Session Outline

Note: Refer to the format templates on pages 7–8 for suggested time allotments.

Welcome

Offer a word of welcome to the group. If time allows and you choose to provide food, invite the women to enjoy refreshments and fellowship. (Groups meeting for 60 minutes may want to have a time for food and fellowship before the official start time.) Be sure to watch the clock and move to the All Play icebreaker at the appropriate time.

All Play

Ask each group member to respond briefly to the following prompt. Read aloud or paraphrase:

- *If you could honor someone publicly, who would it be?*

After everyone has shared, say something like:

Maybe you named a great leader, a famous artist, or a family member who inspires you. While our earthly heroes can provide us great examples to follow, Yahweh reveals that His attributes transcend human accomplishments.

Prayer/Video

Ask God to prepare the group to receive His Word and hear His voice. Play the video for Week 4. Invite participants to complete the Video Viewer Guide for Week 4 in the participant workbook as they watch (page 139). (Answers are provided on page 205 of the participant workbook or page 61 of this leader guide.)

Group Discussion

VIDEO DISCUSSION QUESTIONS

- What circumstances have been stealing your peace lately (*regret from the past, conflict in the present, fear for the future*)?
- What in Gideon's encounter with Yahweh Shalom stands out to you? Why?
- How do you think you can apply the PAT acronym in your daily life (*Prayer, Appeal, Thanksgiving*)?

- What are some tangible ways you worship God (especially during anxious seasons)?

PARTICIPANT WORKBOOK DISCUSSION QUESTIONS

Note: Page references are provided for those questions that relate to questions or activities in the participant workbook.

Before you begin, invite volunteers to look up the following Scriptures and be prepared to read them aloud when called upon. You might want to write each of the Scripture references on a separate index card or sticky note that you can hand out.

Scriptures: Judges 6:22-24; Psalm 23; Jeremiah 23:1-8; Ezekiel 6:7; 36:26-27; John 14:27; 16:33

Day 1: Yahweh Shalom—The Lord Is Peace

- What is causing stress in your life lately, whether something small or a major stressor? (page 109)
- Have someone read Judges 6:22-24. How does knowing that the Lord is not only with us but also for us bring you encouragement today?
- As you reflect on Gideon's story from Judges 6, what principles about peace stand out to you? (page 112)
- Have someone read John 14:27 and John 16:33. What did Jesus promise us in these passages?
- Ask a few individuals to share their statements of belief on page 114.

Day 2: Yahweh Sabaoth—The Lord of Heaven's Armies

- What weather icon did you choose that most closely describes your current life circumstances? Why? (page 115)
- Who was the first biblical character to use God's name Yahweh Sabaoth? What did you learn about Hannah's circumstances and her responses to them?
- What challenging situations have you been facing lately? (page 117)
- As you think about any storms in your life recently or in the past, how have you responded? (page 117)
- Ask a few individuals to share their statements of belief on page 120.

Day 3: Yahweh Raah—The Lord My Shepherd

- Have someone read Psalm 23 out loud. How have these verses brought you comfort in the past? How did they bring comfort today?
- Which of the four benefits of having Yahweh Raah as our Shepherd stood out most to you? (page 125) (*Contentment, Restoration, Guidance, Protection*)
- How has the Lord been a Shepherd in your life?
- What new insights did you glean from learning a shepherd's perspective on Psalm 23?
- As you think about your role as a sheep, are there any steps you could take to cooperate more fully with the care that Yahweh Raah offers you? (page 126)
- Ask a few individuals to share their statements of belief on page 126.

Day 4: Yahweh Tsidkenu—The Lord Is Our Righteousness

- Have someone read aloud Jeremiah 23:1-8 and Ezekiel 36:26-27. From these passages, what do we learn about heart transformation versus behavior modification?
- How does Christ's ministry confirm these teachings of God as Yahweh Tsidkenu? (*He supplies our righteousness; we cannot manufacture it.*)
- How can you relate to the tension between choosing human effort and yielding to divine power in your own practical pursuit of right living this week? (page 130)
- Ask a few individuals to share their statements of belief on page 131.

Day 5: Yahweh Shammah—The Lord Is There

- What comes to your mind as you hear the name Yahweh Shammah, The Lord is There? (page 132)
- Have someone read Ezekiel 6:7. What does this verse reveal as God's purpose behind His judgments?
- How did the verses at the end of Day 5 bring you comfort as they assure us of God's presence in our lives? (pages 135–136)
- As you look back over the entire week, what names of God have resonated most with you, and why?
- Ask if anyone would like to recite the memory verse or share how it impacted her personally.

Optional Group Activity (for a session longer than 60 minutes)

Divide into smaller groups or pairs to review the Weekly Wrap-up (pages 137–138). Ask small groups to share and discuss their wrap-up statements and one or two ways that they will put into practice something they learned from their readings this week.

Prayer Requests

Invite the group members to share prayer requests and pray for one another. Use index cards or sticky notes, popcorn prayer, or another prayer technique included in Tips for Tackling Five Common Challenges (pages 13–19) to lead this time with intentionality and sensitivity.

Week 5

ADONAI, ABBA, HOLY SPIRIT

Adonai, Abba, Ruwach, Holy Spirit-Teacher, Holy Spirit-Comforter

Leader Prep

Memory Verse

"For God is Spirit, so those who worship him must worship in spirit and in truth."

(John 4:24)

Materials Needed

- *The Names of God* DVD and DVD player or equipment to stream the video online
- Stick-on name tags and markers (optional)
- Index cards or sticky notes (optional—Scriptures and Prayer Requests)

Session Outline

Note: Refer to the format templates on pages 7–8 for suggested time allotments.

Welcome

Offer a word of welcome to the group. If time allows and you choose to provide food, invite the women to enjoy refreshments and fellowship. (Groups meeting for 60 minutes may want to have a time for food and fellowship before the official start time.) Be sure to watch the clock and move to the All Play icebreaker at the appropriate time.

All Play

Ask each group member to respond briefly to the following prompt:

- *Name something you can't physically see with your eyes that you are grateful for today. (love, compassion, time, etc.)*

After everyone shares, say:

> *Just because we can't see time, love, or compassion doesn't mean that they aren't real. In the same way, we can't physically see the Holy Spirit, but we know He is working in our hearts.*

Prayer/Video

Ask God to prepare the group to receive His Word and hear His voice. Play the video for Week 5. Invite participants to complete the Video Viewer Guide for Week 5 in the participant workbook as they watch (page 171). (Answers are provided on page 205 of the participant workbook or page 61 of this leader guide.)

Group Discussion

VIDEO DISCUSSION QUESTIONS

- How has the Holy Spirit helped you understand the Bible?
- What would more of the Holy Spirit's influence look like in your everyday life?
- Can you relate to having restlessness in your soul when you have felt like you just needed something? How has the Holy Spirit fulfilled that longing at some point in your life?

- What would it look like for you to listen more attentively to the Holy Spirit?

Participant Workbook Discussion Questions

Note: Page references are provided for those questions that relate to questions or activities in the participant workbook.

Before you begin, invite volunteers to look up the following Scriptures and be prepared to read them aloud when called upon. You might want to write each of the Scripture references on a separate index card or sticky note that you can hand out.

Scriptures: Genesis 15:1-8; Exodus 31:1-5; Mark 14:32-36; John 15:26; Romans 8:15-17; Galatians 5:22-23

Day 1: Adonai—Master

- In what ways do you see followers of Christ allowing God to have control in their lives? (page 141)
- Have someone read Genesis 15:1-8. What stands out to you about the manner in which Abraham addressed the Lord?
- What do the situations of Moses, Joshua, and Gideon have in common? (page 144)
- Can you think of a time in your life when following God's instructions left you with questions? If so, share about it briefly with the group.
- Ask a few individuals to share their statements of belief on page 145.

Day 2: Abba—Father

- In one word, how would you describe your relationship with your dad? (page 146)
- Have someone read aloud Mark 14:32-36. How did you describe the situation when Jesus cried out to God as "Abba, Father"? (page 148)
- Have someone read Romans 8:15-17. How does the truth about your identity as a child of God encourage you today? (page 149)
- Ask a few individuals to share their statements of belief on page 150.

Day 3: Ruwach—The Spirit of God

- Have someone read aloud Exodus 31:1-5. How did the Spirit equip Bezalel? (page 152)

- What did each judge in the three passages from the Book of Judges accomplish through the Spirit of the Lord? (page 152)
- What similarities or differences did you notice between the work of the Holy Spirit in the Old and New Testaments? (page 154)
- Ask a few individuals to share their statements of belief on page 155.

Day 4: Holy Spirit—Teacher

- Where did you first hear about the Holy Spirit, and what initial impressions did you have of Him? (page 157)
- Have someone read Galatians 5:22-23. Based on the fruit of the Spirit listed here, how have you been doing lately with yielding to the Holy Spirit?
- Do you have a story about a time when you sensed the Holy Spirit directing you in some way? If so, share it with the group. (page 160)
- What are some ways we can recognize the voice of the Holy Spirit in our lives? (page 161)
- Ask a few individuals to share their statements of belief on page 162.

Day 5: Holy Spirit—Comforter

- What are some ways we look for comfort when we feel sad or hurt? (page 163)
- Have someone read aloud John 15:26. What did Jesus tell us about the Holy Spirit according to this verse?
- Have you ever sought comfort from God through His Holy Spirit? If so, what are some ways that you have received help in a difficult time? (page 165)
- As you look back over the entire week, what names of God have resonated most with you, and why?
- Ask if anyone would like to recite the memory verse or share how it impacted her personally.

Optional Group Activity (for a session longer than 60 minutes)

Divide into smaller groups or pairs to review the Weekly Wrap-up (pages 169–170). Ask small groups to share and discuss their wrap-up statements and one or two ways that they will put into practice something they learned from their readings this week.

Prayer Requests

Invite the group members to share prayer requests and pray for one another. Use index cards or sticky notes, popcorn prayer, or another prayer technique included in Tips for Tackling Five Common Challenges (pages 13–19) to lead this time with intentionality and sensitivity.

Week 6

Savior, Messiah, Redeemer, I AM, Name above All Names

Leader Prep

Memory Verse

> *Therefore, God elevated him to the place of highest honor*
> *and gave him the name above all other names,*
> *that at the name of Jesus every knee should bow,*
> *in heaven and on earth and under the earth,*
> *and every tongue declare that Jesus Christ is Lord,*
> *to the glory of God the Father.*
>
> (Philippians 2:9-11)

Materials Needed

- The Names of God DVD and DVD player or equipment to stream the video online

- Stick-on name tags and markers (optional)
- Blank cardstock bookmarks and gel pens (optional—Group Activity)
- Index cards or sticky notes (optional—Scriptures and Prayer Requests)

Session Outline

Note: Refer to the format templates on pages 7–8 for suggested time allotments.

Welcome

Offer a word of welcome to the group. If time allows and you choose to provide food, invite the women to enjoy refreshments and fellowship. (Groups meeting for 60 minutes may want to have a time for food and fellowship before the official start time.) Be sure to watch the clock and move to the All Play icebreaker at the appropriate time.

All Play

Ask each group member to respond briefly to the following prompt. Read aloud or paraphrase:

- *What is a task that you wish you had an easy button for right now?*
  (In other words, what is something difficult that you wish could be easier?)

After everyone shares, say something like:

Some things in life have become easier with technology. Streaming our favorite shows on demand and ordering things online have enhanced our ability to get things and entertain ourselves. But some things in life require commitment and hard work. When it comes to deep relationships, healthy eating, and developing spiritual rhythms that will draw us closer to Jesus, there is no instant "easy" button. Yet, often the things that take the most intentionality and focus offer the greatest rewards in return. Pursuing Jesus certainly falls in that category!

Prayer/Video

Ask God to prepare the group to receive His Word and hear His voice. Play the video for Week 6. Invite participants to complete the Video Viewer Guide for Week 6 in the participant workbook as they watch (pages 203). (Answers are provided on page 205 of the participant workbook or page 61 of this leader guide.)

Group Discussion

- What are some tasks you have prioritized on a regular basis?
- How can your knowledge of God's names impact your walk with the Lord?
- Pursuing wholeness requires a willingness to let go. What is the Lord asking you to release to Him in this current season?
- Pursuing wholeness requires clinging to the right one. What would it look like for you to cling tighter to Jesus in practical ways this week?
- Pursuing wholeness requires getting things in the right order. What are some changes you need to make in your life's priorities right now? (Reference the rice and walnuts illustration.)

Participant Workbook Discussion Questions

Note: Page references are provided for those questions that relate to questions or activities in the participant workbook.

Before you begin, invite volunteers to look up the following Scriptures and be prepared to read them aloud when called upon. You might want to write each of the Scripture references on a separate index card or sticky note that you can hand out.

Scriptures: Matthew 1:18-25; 16:13-16; John 6:35; 8:12; 10:7, 11; 11:25; 14:6; 15:1-8; Romans 6:4-14; 2 Corinthians 1:18-20; Hebrews 9:11-28; Philippians 2:1-11

Day 1: Jesus—Savior

- Today when you think of Jesus, how do you picture Him? (page 173)
- Ask someone to read Matthew 1:18-25. What names for Jesus did you encounter in these verses, and what do they mean to you?
- Take a moment to consider where you would be without Jesus. Share with the group how your life might be different without Him. (page 174)
- Read Romans 6:4-14 and share a brief description of how Jesus is our salvation when it comes to our daily choices. (page 175)
- Ask a few individuals to share their statements of belief on page 177.

Day 2: Jesus—Messiah

- What are some ways you would answer the question "Who am I?" in this season of life? (page 178)
- Have someone read Matthew 16:13-16. What questions did Jesus ask?
- What question would you want to ask Jesus if He were sitting next to you right now? (page 180)
- How can you more fully appreciate and utilize the access to God that Jesus provides? (page 181)
- Ask a few individuals to share their statements of belief on page 182.

Day 3: Jesus—Redeemer

- A redeemer serves to restore what has been lost. What are some losses you have experienced in your life? (page 184)
- Have someone read aloud Hebrews 9:11-28. What are some truths that stand out to you about Christ's role as a Redeemer? (page 186)
- How does knowing that Christ is a Redeemer encourage you today? (page 187)
- Ask a few individuals to share their statements of belief on page 188.

Day 4: Jesus—I AM

- Have several volunteers read aloud John 6:35; John 8:12; John 10:7; John 10:11; John 11:25; and John 14:6. Which of these "I AM" statements stands out most to you today? Why? (page 190)
- If you know Jesus, how has He helped you sort out truth in your life? (page 191)
- Have someone read John 15:1-8. What does remaining in Jesus look like—practically—for you today? (page 193)
- Ask a few individuals to share their statements of belief on page 194.

Day 5: Jesus—Name above All Names

- Have someone read aloud Philippians 2:1-11. In what ways could the Lord be calling you to take the humble posture of Christ in some of your current circumstances? (page 196)
- Have someone read aloud 2 Corinthians 1:18-20. How does knowing that Jesus is "Yes and Amen" give you encouragement or direction in your life right now? (page 196)

- As you look back over the entire week, what names of Jesus have resonated most with you, and why?
- Ask if anyone would like to recite the memory verse or share how it impacted her personally.
- As you reflect on our study of God's names, what has stood out most to you? What did you star on the summary chart? (pages 198–201)

Optional Group Activity (for a session longer than 60 minutes)

To close your study, hand out blank cardstock bookmarks and set out some gel pens or colored pencils. Ask participants to reflect on the memory verses and main points they've studied over the last six weeks, and invite them to write on their bookmarks a favorite memory verse, word, or quote from a daily reading. If you have time, ask some volunteers to share what they wrote and why.

Prayer Requests

Invite the group members to share prayer requests and pray for one another. Use index cards or sticky notes, popcorn prayer, or another prayer technique included in Tips for Tackling Five Common Challenges (pages 13–19) to lead this time with intentionality and sensitivity. Give thanks for all that you have learned and experienced together, and ask God to help you share the good news you've studied with others in the coming weeks.

Video Viewer Guide Answers

Introductory Video
better / better
Behold
Believe
Bloom
essential picture
El
Yahweh
Trinity
salvation
trust
glory

Week 1
cares / you
big picture
details

Week 2
sufficiency / dependency
relationship
provision
mercy
blessing

Week 3
past / present
vertical
vision
vulnerabilities

Week 4
peace / receive
peace
worship / worry

Week 5
people / power
Someone
expectantly
attentively
Surrender

Week 6
let go
right One
right order

NOTE

1. Dave and Jon Ferguson, *Exponential: How You and Your Friends Can Start a Missional Church Movement* (Grand Rapids, MI: Zondervan, 2010), 58, 63.

Printed in the USA
CPSIA information can be obtained
at www.ICGtesting.com
LVHW081034220724
786153LV00013B/166